Lost in the Foreground

Also by Stephen Edgar
Corrupted Treasures (1995)
Where the Trees Were (1999)

Stephen Edgar

Lost in the Foreground

PICARO PRESS

in loving memory of

Ann Jennings

The author gratefully acknowledges that this project was assisted by
the Australian Government through the Australia Council, its arts
funding and advisory body.

Lost in the Foreground
ISBN 978 1 920957 53 7
Copyright © text Stephen Edgar 2003

First published 2003 by Duffy & Snellgrove

This edition published 2017 by
Picaro Press – an imprint of
GINNINDERRA PRESS
PO Box 3461 Port Adelaide 5015 Australia
www.ginninderrapress.com.au

Contents

The Complete Works	7
The Sea and the City	9
Historians	10
Contents Page	12
In Parenthesis	14
Incident at Grantley Manor	15
The Spies of God	18
Unattended	20
The Book of the Dead	22
Strange Music	26
A Divine Comedy	28
Arcadia	31
Silk Screen	35
Holbein's Skull	38
Stranger to Fiction	40
Ardglen	44
The Customs Officer	46
The Book of Changes	50
Other Friezes	52
Entropy Blues	54
The Company	56
Ghostworkers*	61
The Shadow Maker	63
Midas	65
Sun Pictorial	69
The Single Chamber	71
Signs of Life	73
Fantasia on a Theme by Thomas Tallis	76
Observations of an Attendant	78
Day Work	81
Elemental	83

If truth in hearts that perish
  Could move the powers on high,
I think the love I bear you
  Should make you not to die.

– A. E. Housman, *A Shropshire Lad*, XXXIII

The Complete Works

Over the city's basin, clouds progress:
Continents, Himalayas which bear down
Tectonic force, then evanesce;
Iguaçu Falls
Of turbulent dark marble which would drown
Oblivious dreamers in their flimsy walls,
But lack the gravity of their excess

And are shrugged off by foothills. One immense
Atomic tree form lifts its roiling bole,
Gripping the roofs of residence
It blows asunder,
While in its canopy tumble and roll
The smithereens of suburbs which lie under
That swelling umbrage: world-ash in either sense.

Such scenes of life and death – all make-believe,
An atmospheric horseplay flung together
That fifteen minutes can't retrieve.
The elements
Don't know their elements. They make bad weather.
A wind from nowhere just as soon invents
The evening's empty, lemon-lit reprieve.

Here by the window in the fuchsia's top,
A little wattlebird hangs, acrobatic,
Whose feathered tongue-tip probes to mop
The silly drug
Of its high spirits up. With instamatic
Eyes, it keeps taking snaps, the shutterbug,
Of fantasies that drift and rise and drop

Within the surface of that doubtful mirror:
The marbled sky's distant and vague champaign,
The see-through garden and this clearer
Twin; or it pores
On what the window's stranger deeps contain –
A figure drowning in interiors
Who sometimes floats up menacingly nearer.

What can it know of the image which adheres
To a page inside a book on that man's shelf
(Its own image, so it appears)
Which can attest
More detailed knowledge than the bird itself
Of where and what it is? Who could have guessed
This world it's flying through was once Shakespeare's?

Now fast within themselves the couples lie,
While through this autumn night the lightless cloud
Above their beds breeds in the sky
Vast Yggdrasils,
And earthly trees in darkness, bird-endowed,
Attempt to memorise a wind that spills
From the salt water, making the same cry.

What can they know, as pictures and remarks
Seed in their heads, occasionally to flower
In a dark endearment, or the quirks
Of eye and limb,
About their bodies' other plans, the power
That writes their names, their hidden homonym,
Simple as clouds and birds, complete as Shakespeare's works?

The Sea and the City

Scientists diving off the Florida coast
Have harvested an Indian treasure trove
From that once wide savanna, which a host
Of artless fishes glide clear fathoms above,

Reversing Marvell's marvellous conceit
Of walkers toiling through a submarine
Expanse of grass they fathom with their feet.
One thinks of Celtic myth, of cities seen

Far down in the glassy bell jar of a lake,
Of Ys and of *la cathédrale engloutie,*
Those leagues in which East Anglia lost its stake
To rival claims of the oblivious sea.

But here the city stakes its claim, those hopes
Of steel and concrete which it means to keep,
An eschatology sure as the pope's
That its citizens believe in in their sleep.

Look where the buildings stand and face the slant
Of oceanic sunset they rise through,
Their oriented walls as radiant
As a lover at a lovers' rendezvous.

Since this is all there is for them, it must
Be all there is. Conjecture they discard.
No article of faith need be discussed.
No one intends to give up one square yard.

Historians

Here through the hotel window: hills like hessian
Heaped over there across the river's throng
Of Chinese sparklers, a light breeze to freshen
The sky's one pastel page, that palimpsest
Rubbed back, on which the gulls, attempting song,
Fall to inscribing with a strident zest
The unimproved few notes in their possession.

Some guests are coming out with tennis gear,
Or teeing off at mini golf, or strolling
Along the foreshore anywhere they reach.
Their lips, as in a silent film from here,
Still practise the incongruous but cajoling
Mannerisms of superfluous speech.
The pictures say it all. So much is clear:

They've set themselves among the universals.
Photographs that will be their memories,
Memories that persist in photographs,
Will prove them, after years and their dispersals,
Once ranged among these old topographies
Of light. Easy to read and to reprise
Stories they're now committing to first drafts:

Discoveries, or inventions, of new passion;
Some brief deceit lit with a cigarette
That elsewhere, later, will be largely ashen;
Kinder attachments the free days beget,
Relations made. And you, omniscient
Relater of these narratives, who yet
Know nothing, you are nodding your assent.

Here is the site where history will unfold.
Here are the futures destined to attend it.
And this, your own, so flawed, so unconsoled,
Resistant to revision and controlled
By no director, with no script to quote
No order, plot or lesson to commend it,
Which you can feel now thickening in your throat.

Contents Page

The jungle, from the floor to the canopy,
        Clogs and entwines
Its every rung and level with rank growth.
        The python dines
Among an epiphytic gaudery
        And hungry vines.
On the mizzled hair of the two-toed sloth
        Moss has designs.
Yet all that climbing tonnage is content-free.
The top limbs sway as though to write in air,
But can't remember what they scribble there.

Through the savanna's heat glaze the herds pause,
        Ripple and shiver,
Or graze hypnotically, or drop their young,
        Which may deliver
Their wet thin steps into the lion's jaws.
        By pool or river
They stoop at evening side by side among
        The surface quiver
Of their reflexions as the light withdraws:
A fable set down in invisible ink;
They print their shadows on the pool they drink.

Even the perfect pictures in the shale's
        Slow-motion traps,
The filamentous feathers, which one or two
        Sharp hammer taps
Release, the fish in their meticulous scales,
        The precise maps
Of leaves, did not direct this rendezvous.
        They're simply gaps
In time, and have no part in these details.
The weird wiwaxias, worms and arthropods
Were empty of intention as stone gods.

Once, though, a figure had the thought to crawl
        Out of the day
Into a cave's dark reach, its first invoker,
        And there to splay
His hand against the tallow-glimmered wall,
        And pause to spray
His mouth's cargo of spittle and red ochre
        On the array
Of his five fingers, clear, indelible:
Author and content of the space displayed,
The maker's hand becoming what it made.

In Parenthesis

Beyond night and the elementary moon
The Horse Head Nebula proliferates
Its mindless zeros, like the coral's strewn
And moon-slick spawn. The mud lays down its slates
(A glistening bubble, as in a cartoon,
Appears here out of nowhere and inflates
With wild surmise, some fragments of a tune,
Eidola from imaginary fates,

Millennial desires, hypotheses
Of sense, until its infinite cubic inch
Contains again everything it divides)
And afternoon's chromatic harmonies
Play on, through which, unpuzzled, flits the finch
And the wind-proud raptor without question glides.

Incident at Grantley Manor

Seven o'clock, the time set in his mind
Like herbs displayed in aspic, as the chimes
Were striking. Then the squeaking of his shoes'

Black leather tread, pacing those measures down
The first-floor hall, where sunset's apricot
Was oozing nectar through the open doors.

Her voice, conspiratorial and astonished,
Called him across the bedroom's drowning cube
Towards the window. How well Miss Waterson

Remembers it: 'Please come and look at this,
Mr Devine'; the clock on the mantelpiece
Rehearsing for the hour of seven. She pointed

Down. There, a moving picture on the lawn,
His father, like a patient whose long months
Of immobility meant learning afresh

The art of walking, climbing the light's green slope
Towards the summer house, looking intently
As though for a cuff link or a signature.

That evening he still thinks of, lying now,
No longer needing lessons for his legs,
How he cast back his glance and saw the windows

Blazing like cats' eyes on his uselessness,
And in that golden mirror, two gold figures
Recording him, two shadows of dark gold –

Miss Waterson (was it?) and another one –
And then took out his watch on which the hands
Were so meticulously assembling seven.

Young Emily, appointed just the week
Before, came rushing to the stairs – she'd seen
Him stumble – to advise Mr Devine

About his father's fall. And so, almost
Immobilised herself in that clinging syrup,
She observed the hall clock's quaint rendition of

Seven, the time set clearly in his mind
Like summer herbs in aspic, as the chimes
Were striking. Then the squeaking of his shoes'

Black leather tread, pacing those measures down
The corridor, where sunset's apricot
Was oozing nectar through the open doors.

Her voice, companionable but astonished,
Floated across the bedroom's drowning cube
As he descended. How well Miss Waterson

Remembers it: 'Please come and look at this';
And Emily, who had just been taken on
That week, came rushing to the window. She pointed

Down, smartly on the stroke of seven. There,
A moving picture on the lawn, was old
Mr Devine, like a patient whose long months

Of immobility meant learning afresh
The art of walking, climbing the light's green slope
Abstractedly towards the rose garden.

That evening he still thinks of, lying now,
No longer needing lessons for his legs,
How he cast back his glance and saw the windows

Glaring like cats' eyes on his helplessness,
And in that golden mirror, two gold figures
Gesticulating, two shadows of dark gold –

The new girl (was it?) and another one –
And then took out his watch on which the hands
Were so laboriously assembling seven.

Miss Waterson, with Emily behind her
In a panic, dashed to the stairs to find
Mr Devine, anxious to let him know

About his father's fall. And there they saw him,
Almost immobile in that clinging syrup,
And heard the hall clock's muffled tolling of

Seven, the time set firmly in his mind…

The Spies of God

As though one had to travel to Galveston
To prise a flake of duco
Out of the jagged puzzle of a crash

(When once upon a time and place, one glance,
Even a simpleton's
Almost a babe-in-arms', or any man's

Cast in the midst of daylight's disarray,
Might take in and acknowledge,
Without the need to put it into words

Or conscious thought, this complex gift. And so
It ought to be, one might
Suppose: one sweep of unencumbered sight

Setting the stone, the shadow of the pine,
The crow's caw and the smell
Of bread in disposition); then to Seville

To pluck the soiled down from a swallow's nest;
In London to seek out
On Portobello Road a silver egg cup;

The aglet from a businessman's black shoelace
Next year in Marienbad;
In Riyadh, say, an alif from a page

Of newsprint. But all this would be child's play.
More telling the condition
To gather in the rhythms of a rosebush

Against a lattice in a breeze, one cool
Spring day in Trebizond;
The intonations of Etruscan speech;

The various lights of noon on May the third
In all the successive years
Of one anonymous, elusive life;

The lost sensations of a stillborn child;
The innumerable faces
Which crowd the surface of unvisited sleep.

But why go on? Why plait these ropes of air?
With all these tesserae
These scraps, labilities and whispers, he

Who found these riddles out, yes, even he
Would be but a messenger,
And only one among the mutually

Unrecognisable company dispersed
Through accidental cities,
The far-flung centuries; and he would sleep

As ignorant as all in his brief room
While bits and pieces of
That image spilled their powders in his desk,

Or wake as in a dream to find himself
Required to read a script
Of cuneiform, the figures in a carpet,

Or squatting in the square, like a simpleton
Before the mocking crowd,
Move nothings in the dust with his bare hands.

Unattended

Here is unfenced existence

The scene of an incessant,
Elaborately orchestrated looting
Lies on the city like an eternal present –
A kind of paradise
Transmuting
The insubstantial pageant to precise
And wrapped requirements, from runners to rice.

Dull-eyed inhabitants
Of close unlively suburbs shove and buff
Along the aisles – as though they moved in trance –
Their glutted trolleyfuls
Of stuff,
Their appetite so freighted as it schools
Them through the ranked and packaged multiples

Of goods too good to miss,
They have, it seems, no urge left to rebel,
Like Milton's Lucifer, from the rules of bliss.
Far off, below the treed
Hills, dwell
More subtle others whose exertions feed
On grand views that no rival may impede,

On living space as wide
As showrooms and on terraced frontages.
Down sinuous driveways cars serenely glide.
On smooth lawn cycles sprawl.
There is
A dome of silence settled over all
These places to both privilege and enthral.

Beyond the last of them
The droughty headland, long deforested,
Abandoned to its larks and the dry-stem
Grass, goes on unattended,
Unfed
In windy light. The seedheads sway suspended
Like hosts of banners till the land is ended.

Across the upper slope
A raven drops its shadow down to plumb
Some gully hidden among shades of taupe
And grey, trailing a yell.
A gum,
A lifetime dead, which they forgot to fell,
May call a kestrel up for sentinel.

A flat wind strokes the grasses
The wrong way like a cat's fur, or the pile
Of carpet sheening back where a foot passes.
All parched and silver-pressed,
Stalks file
Or flow uphill, to spill over the crest
A waterfall that only falls unwitnessed.

The sea breeze pushes flakes
Of sun like flotsam deep into the bay,
A process that won't stop and only makes
Itself; the wavelets churn
Away
With Brownian coruscation, in which burn
And burn the phoenix gulls and then return.

The Book of the Dead

Only the later voyage had revealed
What none of us could have imagined then,
Setting our feet the first time in that realm
Of prodigies and marvels:
Such butterflies as seemed kaleidoscopes,
The colours in their wings never the same
From moment to moment; and if you held your hand
Palm upward in the light, in which would pool
A nectarous quintessence, luminously
Distilled out of the air, they'd come and perch
Like tame birds on your thumb and sip it up.
Their wings' sheer voile, as wide as looking glasses
In the floating wind, might fleetingly display
Dim visions out of time. And so their own
Intoxicated priests would prophesy
From intermittent glimpses, intimations,
Reading the signals of their brilliant flight,
Interpreting that iridescent theatre.

A flower there was which bloomed only on nights
Of the full moon, unfurling shudderingly
A broad two-petalled blossom, which would stare
Above at its reflexion posed on high.
But if one who desired foreknowledge of
A future love, or the identity
Of some ill-willed opponent who had worked
Him harm, should stretch out underneath the bud
And fall asleep in full thought of his wish,
The flower would open and bend heavily
Towards him, while across its pale expanse

The features of the culprit or his lover
Would rise, like welts or decorative markings
On the skin, and hang there till just after dawn
To meet the sleeper's first awakening gaze,
Then wither up and drop.

Some trees had liquid gold for sap, or silver,
And this the indigenes would milk by means
Of small incisions in the bark, or snipping
Tips of the new leaves, out of which it oozed
Like honey from the comb. These sacred trees
They kept from us, nor would they let us drink,
But we observed how one drop on the tongue
Dissolved its rapture and
Transfigured them before our envious eyes.

They knew a bird whose eggs, one in a thousand
Maybe, would yield a gem, just as a pearl
Grows in an oyster, and on the evening of
The vernal equinox the women…
Such riches we might well have coveted
And made our claim for King and Christendom.
But when their wise men saw the quills we dipped
And watched the dark enigmas they poured forth
Unprompted, coastlines out of memory magicked
Onto parchment scrolls,
They grew afraid, some fleeing, lost for words,
Into the green thesaurus of the trees;
Others grew sullen and belligerent.

But we had our own calendar. We sailed
Away into the world with our reports,
Our maps and tables. Theirs, we would have thought,
Was all the prophecy, theirs the domain
That undid nature's writ, theirs were the gifts
That might commune with and administer death.

Years after, sailing back the second time,
Calling by conjuration of our charts
Their islands into being, we waited for
The uproar from their tribes, but only found
Silent hamlets one after another,
Or sickly groups in twos and threes, reluctant
And without a word for us.

Later, when we were anchored and encamped
Along that hushed shore, cautious, solitary,
A man from years before approached, and him
We could persuade to speak.
What was the plague? A mere coincidence?
A vapour or contagion we had brought
Unwittingly before? Some unforeseen
Effect of the food and drink that we had let
Them taste? All these the envoy waved away,
Pointing in awe towards the writing desk
In view behind me in my tent, the journal
Laid open to the day.
'The feather that sheds blood,' he said to us.

'The skin that it tattoos. Only when
You put our people down upon your page
And caught the words we uttered out of the air,
Like butterflies, making them black designs
Without a voice, which named in silence all
Our lives and stories – it was only then
That we began to die.'

Strange Music

A group of wailing, black-clad women stands
In grief's inductive trance.
The river bears their loved one off. Their hands
Flap, though hysterically, to the beat
Of an unheard music, while their naked feet
Fulfil the rhythms of slow dance.

Egypt: some former ordering of matters,
Or magic, still holds sway.
And, working through their hearts, draws in the tatters,
The grief-torn scraps of a terrain
No word of theirs has power to sustain,
And lets it live for one more day.

In a stone gloom the lion god's displayed
(The tourists with their brief
Attention flicker past) – tear marks inlaid
Deep in the corners of his eyes;
His face is leonine and sadly wise,
His human body swaddling-stiff.

Then too the powers hardly allowed for words:
The presence in the stone,
The presage in the motion of the birds,
Recurrence of the sun that fed
The everlasting banquet of the dead,
The signal in the jackal's bone.

Out on the molten river craft obey
Miraculous new conditions,
Although the old wind plays with them all day
And fills the lateen sails, although
The ancient waters still contrive to flow:
The new rules of the new magicians,

The truth that shocks all those who've understood
(And who can understand?) –
A magic stranger than the lion god.
Back home the tourists with their brief
Attention flicker past the new belief.
Their hearts are still in Egypt, and

The unheard music and the wailing cry
Those women clad in black
Raise up distract them, while the magics vie
To hear the presence in the stone,
To see the signal in the jackal's bone,
To know what makes the sun come back.

A Divine Comedy

1. Inferno

Death comes with the archbishop after luncheon.
Instruments of salvation are displayed.
His Grace, with fluent words of extreme unction,
Absolves the civic saint from a crusade
Waged beyond hope of doubt. His children kneel,
Like problems yet to solve, around the chosen,
Whose death is, like his life, now past appeal,
Though not (they pray) their prayers. The scene is frozen,

And in the brief hiatus of this hush
The artist dabs one last reflective glint
Onto the canvas, then lays down his brush
And quits the studio. Daylight's vestigial
Radiance goes out too, taking the hint,
And leaves the night to keep its long black vigil.

2. Purgatorio

The PM with a sudden change of plan
Flies out to the doleful city to present,
In private, his farewell to the public man,
A gesture with more meaning than he meant.
In whispered tones, then, on both sides they speak
The words required of them. The family
Sits hovering like a chorus from the Greek,
Concerned and helpless and compulsory.

The scene completed, the actors all depart
This final dress rehearsal. Silence falls,
But for some faint retreating steps and chatter,
On what was here committed to the heart.
A backdrop sways and looks out on the stalls.
No house lights come on in the empty theatre.

3. Paradiso

The service of the State is done, and while
The incense and the floating prayers disperse,
His flag-wrapped coffin glides along the aisle
Out to the autumn sunshine and the hearse.
Along the street spontaneous applause
Pours from the honest populace, who sway
Towards the vehicle as it withdraws
Like a black magnet through them and the day.

But from a sidelong angle can be seen
A shaft of flickering multicoloured light
Projecting through the auditorium
Onto the fabric of the floating screen
These weightless animations, till they come
To their conclusion and the screen goes white.

Arcadia

in memory of Gwen Harwood

Out in the middle of
A Sunday afternoon
And empty Oyster Cove
Where mottled sky was strewn
      In gloss and matt,
We rode the smack and slide
      Of wavelets at
The dinghy's dipping side,

Dragging the flathead out
As though they came when called
Without demur or doubt.
Triumphantly we hauled
      Our silver hoard
On board, then turned to row
      Stiffly toward
The shoreline's silver flow.

A simple tale enough.
Yet such a mundane guise
Concealed the very stuff
You would memorialise
      Almost before
The moment slipped away,
      And so restore
That day to a later day.

The merest hour we spent
In your strange alchemy
Would, on a subsequent
Occasion, prove to be
   Bathed in so gold
A radiance of fond
   Recall retold,
It would scarcely correspond

With what we thought had been.
So richly did you bring
To any foregone scene
Desire's transfiguring,
   That the career
Of fearful time might yield
   Its cargo here,
To lie stilled and distilled.

Things to delight a child:
Wildflowers, a meal, your hens,
Or Bruny's hills beguiled
By light, shone in that lens.
   But shadows too
Darkened Arcadia.
   None more than you
Knew where the shadows are.

The simplest questions cast
A shade in which we're numb.
We can recall the past;
Why not what is to come?
        We do not fear
The oblivion before
        Our coming here;
Why that which is in store?

When one that we love dies
With childlike panic we
Are forced to realise
The vast simplicity
        Of waiting pain
In which the heart is hurled.
        Never again
In the story of the world

Will this person appear.
We look for the known face,
Imagine it is near.
But there is just a space
        We can't ignore
And neither can appease,
        In which we pour
Our grief and memories.

Like the still centre of
That Sunday afternoon
In empty Oyster Cove
Where scenes the sky had strewn
        Were glossed and matted
On water, and our lines
        Dragged up the flathead,
Shattering light's designs.

And that was your last wish:
If given back one day,
To go after the fish;
With death to lift away
        From the shore and,
Borne up by sealight, flow
        From the stilled land
In silence. It was so.

Silk Screen

Furnished across a table,
The long provisions of midafternoon:
The cups, according as each tongue is able
To stand the heat, more or less full, and strewn
About a slewed and wrinkled
Expanse of damask that is crumb-besprinkled

With biscuit, scone and cake,
Freighted with plates and variously stained.
A gathering suffused with the slight ache
Of an old familial boredom, unexplained,
Transacted intimately.
Behind the group the windowed estuary,

Which until now had been
Delayed among such subtleties as those
Played out inside, too dull to make a scene,
Emerges from its featureless repose.
Now as the winter light
Sinks yet one more degree into respite,

Its talcum powder greys,
Ranked far towards the city, screen on screen,
Bewitchingly detain what they erase,
Assembling a new scene from the unseen,
So that the pooled and pleated
Spread of river, tree stencils, mist-deleted

Bluffs and bays, the tiers
Of suburbs from the foreshore's basque of foam
Up to the foothills – everything inheres
Ghosted behind a wash of monochrome.
A shadow light invades
Cloud, water, slopes: so many Chinese grades

Of columbine and pearl,
Layered against a parquetry of pewter,
Gunmetal plates and sheets of faded merle.
Uncolours lost to colour, rendered neuter
(A glintless skyey sheen
Of eau de nil that is bankrupt of green,

A Copenhagen blue
Deprived of blue), obsessing concentration
By drawing each declared outline and hue
Into a hushed grisaille of intimation.
Through mantling of matt silk
Seeps a pine rumour. Drowned in shadowed milk,

Loomings ride up and swim
Of breath-faint hulls and mastheads. Over there on
The docks, some gantry stain behind the scrim
Stands groping. Steeped in day, a half-guessed heron
Silently intercedes
Among the lead-lit shallows where it feeds.

And now, melting as if
Oozed from the river's deep to its bleared bank,
One solitary blush mark, a rose glyph
Of sun, escapes the cloud on the mountain's flank
And instantly instils
A drop of dye that quickens where it spills.

Absorbed into the screen
They're ranged against, the figures face to face,
Sipping and mumbling cake, chatting between
Mouthfuls, become still shadows at its base
To at least one pair of eyes,
For which the window mounts its final guise.

The sun cannot resist
Showing the flag of imperial Japan
(Except translucent, moted with the mist),
Whose bars of apricot and salmon fan
That band of liquor which
Their deepening audacities enrich.

The river's ash and nacre
Are flooded where the crimsons grow across,
And as those figures dim to simulacra
Tableaued in black, the screen redeems its loss,
Ransoming in red
The colours afternoon had forfeited.

Holbein's Skull

    Blotting the mountainside,
A bushfire's smoke rolls its appalling frieze,
Its *Gates of Hell,* so simply eloquent.
Now, black as an eclipse, it's gone,
Now the nocturnal city parodies
    The Milky Way, wide-eyed
        And innocent.
Like a child's practice with the alphabet,
    Big letters stand up on
The blackboard of the sky, in dazzling yet
    Child-simple primaries.

    Housed in one window are
The haunted scenes which fill the attendant viewer
With half-held love, a grasped incomprehension:
Now teeming in the morning light
Where perfect figures, modelled in miniature
    By Bosch, play their bizarre,
        Their old invention;
Now emptied afternoon in a gold glare
    Of Turner's; and now the night
With its late-Rembrandt glooms cast back to where
    The doubtful paramour

    Looks on. Or more than these?
That elongated shadow, is that the clue,
A further image sprawling across these scenes,
Like Holbein's anamorphic skull
In *The Ambassadors,* so painted through
    The shades and brilliancies,
        And which so leans
Aslant, some other optic must obtain
    To make it visible
Than these plain eyes, or this one window's plane
    And simply offered view?

Stranger to Fiction

for Connie Rose Smee

'…like one newly born who sees [the world] for the first time, when it still has the air of fiction. It lasts one day.' – Saul Steinberg

      Dear love, look here:
A naked couple couched inside
      A glassy sphere,
Tender and self-preoccupied.
      Clearly, they have no wish to hide.

      About them swarms
A multifarious multitude,
      Their perfect forms
Also preoccupied, and nude,
      In pastimes innocent and lewd.

      Birds larger than
We'd hope to come across are there.
      One feeds a man
A monstrous berry. But beware:
      He's turning purple as we stare.

      And every kind
Of animal, imaginary
      And true, we find
Ambling about the landscape, free
      And tame – or so they seem to be.

      In and around
A sportive lake, which occupies
      The distant ground,
The most bizarre structures arise,
      Prodigious in their shape and size –

    And in their poise,
Daringly balanced in the view
        Like giant toys,
Part castle, sculpture, weapon, screw,
        Part fungus, and part lobster too.

    In the far sky
Strange creatures (can this be a dream?)
        And people fly.
Even a fish. Berries do seem
        Important to this odd regime.

    So on it goes
In ordered pandemonium.
        Well might you close
Your shocked blue eyes and suck your thumb.
        That man's got flowers up his bum.

    But all this rife
And risqué riot's only art.
        This is not life.
From that I'd save you, for my part,
        If I knew how to; cross my heart.

    Well might your blue
And shocked eyes hide away behind
        Your eyelids (too
Translucent, it would seem, to blind
        The daylight out, frailly designed

        With filaments
Of arteries, flicking in sleep
        With inner sense).
Well might your hand minutely grip
        One adult stable fingertip,

        While you delay
A little longer all the sights
        That will betray
You from your perinatal rights
        Into this garden of delights.

        In this strange land
The light comes on and off each day.
        A man may stand
On two feet and not float away.
        One word has many things to say.

        Oh yes, out there
What water stretches it may shrink.
        The absent air
Will stroke your face and make you blink.
        The world is odder than you think.

        Mirrors look deep.
Dark shadows grow in the sun's beams.
        Shut out by sleep,
The day sneaks back again in dreams.
        The world is stranger than it seems.

    And in this weird
Hallucination and cartoon
        You have appeared,
A stranger too, though not immune
            To habit's house rules. All too soon

        Each magic form,
Conjured out of the air, will be
        The daily norm.
Then cherish, retrospectively,
            This moment lost to memory.

        Soon, Connie Rose,
You'll read the fictions on display,
        And after those,
You'll make up, it is safe to say,
            Some fictions of your own one day.

        The day's begun
(Though this day you will not retrieve).
        Under the sun
You'll gather as you learn to grieve
            Things that you would not now believe.

Ardglen

Like gazing at some other family
In a fogged window pane,
Or in a mottled mirror that has lost
Flakes of its silver tain:

The four boys head and tail in the one bed,
Their breath turning the room's
Frigid midwinter to a dreaming kitchen,
With its fug of steam and fumes.

Does such a place exist? Where might it be?
How get to here from there?
But there they are, there *we* are, clambering down
The bank, our thin legs bare,

Barefoot (it's hard to credit) in that cold.
My sook-soft soles revealed,
I'm piggybacked by one of my cousins over
The thorns that mine the field,

Till we reach the dingy creek to fish up yabbies
On strings of sodden meat,
And lug back home our squirming bucketful –
Which of course no one will eat.

Over it goes, then, in the yard; we watch
Them spill and clatter away
Through grass and fence and blackberries, back to
Their soupy deep. One day

We ranged the paddocks – to the quarry (was it?)
Across the railway line,
And tightropewalked the daring empty tracks,
Or, listening for a sign,

We'd place an ear down on the sun-cold metal
And think we heard the humming,
That charged vibration borne from far away
Of what was coming.

The Customs Officer

But always when the occasion comes again,
Like Kafka's keeper of the door, he's there,
To quiz you yet again, or to detain:

Forever that inveterate questionnaire,
Those statements rather, for he knows all this
Already. This is all an old affair

Between you two – and another whom you miss.
This is a drama with an ancient name,
The script is sacred, and the dramatis

Personae. So you can't hold him to blame;
With what he knows of you, with what you are,
What choice has he? Wouldn't you do the same?

He scans your ticket, consults the calendar,
And checks your papers for the hidden flaws,
One fault that will permit him to debar

You – muttering about a missing clause?
No, murmuring as he scribbles to endorse
Your form. You read it now: 'No cause. No cause.'

He lets you pass, though it seems to reinforce
Your sense the visa is provisional.
And ever and anon the normal course,

All unforewarned, some day or place, will haul
You back before him. Now he's going through
Your luggage, searching every article.

'I've lost my mother,' you hear your voice on cue.
You feel a child, although you don't look young.
There's no one left here now but him and you.

He lifts out of your suitcase, from among
Your things, a small plain wooden box, hingeless,
It seems, as airtight as an aqualung.

'This gift,' he starts – the rest, though, you can guess –
'Alone has power to save you from this fate,
These constant calls before me to confess,

These constant reassessments. Listen.' Wait:
You move your ear to the box. A distant breeze
Through grasses sown in summer's lost estate.

'But for owning such a gift, the penalty's
Precisely what it saves you from, no less,
Alas: these constant reassessments, these

Constant calls before me to confess.'
He knows you lied. For when it is not him,
It is that other one, your auditress,

Lying in afternoon's grey interim
With face averted – it's her you're brought before.
'Pray you now, forget and forgive,' her dim

And disembodied words to you implore,
Though no voice can be heard except your own
Forever calling down the corridor

Of shadow. Conjured from the telephone,
The earnest doctor writes: 'No cause. No cause.'
Sometimes you touch her shoulder to atone,

Or try to see her face, but it withdraws,
And nothing's left for you but the faint light
Spilling across the pillow like a pause

In time, the imprint of your leaning height.
'Weep not. Weep not.' For there are interstrewn
Occasions of the gift. Did you, in spite

Of contradictory evidence, one June
Not find yourself on a train through Adlestrop,
The unrecorded stranger that afternoon

Who stepped onto the platform at the stop?
And when the train left with your vacant seat
You lingered listening to summer's crop,

The willows, willowherb, and meadowsweet,
The burry voices of the heat-filled grass
More piercing than the blackbirds in the heat.

One stem you set inside the box. It was
A token for your customs officer,
A proof of faith, an all-resolving pass

Which would undo his power to defer
Your entry, to rescind or to excise.
But when you came on it again, you were

Unable to locate the lid, or prise
It open, so that he might duly find
The gift which only he could authorise,

And placed it in your case, and out of mind.

The Book of Changes

When first they told you – your initiation –
Or you first learned, the look in their eyes betrayed,
Along with a compulsory pride, the addict's
Or criminal's faint leer and half-relief
At having recruited one more to the fold.
A photograph, a shirt, a watch, a view
From a particular room, or reminiscence,
The story of lost years in a neutral city
Now reconstructed or renamed, the privilege
Of a privately numinous word, its intimate
Fore-echoes through your life, the taste inside
A mouth, a body crouched above you webbed
In shadow, a death too soon to be obliged,
So long forestalled that grief is stretched threadbare:
So many tokens of exchange. And money;
Let us, please God, never forget the money.

Any of these might be your payment, or
The payment that is due to you, and in
No single one lies any diminution
Of the knowledge that your life will see no end
Of these transactions, or be other than
Their sum and their perpetual succession.
The timing is unpredictable, perhaps
Pure chance, except that soon or late will come
That next occasion, somewhere obvious
And disappointingly mundane, a shop,
A bus, or least expected, a bush walk,
Or conversation with a faded aunt
One Boxing Day. The rules, which constitute
A masterpiece of obliquity, spell out
This only: nothing given or received
Cancels your debt, the real merchandise.

Who are the guarantors who underwrite
Or valorise these long negotiations?
You've seen the bankers and the visible pact:
I promise to pay the bearer... Pay with what?
And who shall guarantee the guarantors?
There was a time when men exchanged love for love.
Now the nameless gnomes of Zurich have decamped,
The scandal of their absence redirected
To the Atlas Mountains or the Sea of Showers.
Sometimes an image is superimposed upon
These barterings, or comes alone – a dream
Or sentimental passion of the newly
In love, though even this may be no more
Than another surreptitiously encoded
Exchange – a figure, epicene and clothed
To strangeness by the light, intensely holding
Some hidden thing in hands cupped to the breast,
Like escaping water grabbed at by a child,
Or light itself, or merely holding's gesture
All unencumbered by the downward tug
Of matter, meant for you, indefinitely
Withheld, the giving of which might once have cancelled
The rules that line your face and have dogged the years
You've spent in their fulfilment, but can no more,
Impatient as you are, belated and
Complicit in too long a history
Of mutual postponement, which you've paid,
And have been paid, to tell quite otherwise.

Other Friezes

Time enough
To worry about the future
When it's gone.
Those pictures needn't weep
Or teach us how;
They haven't happened yet,
However poignant
In their golden light.
You have, and look
How hardened you've become
To all of this
Strange flux you're moulded to,
The daylight's daily
Sundial, long stuck
Like a painted shadow
On the stroke of disappointment,
Your falling short.

The family
About the evening meal,
Surreally,
Back views form every angle,
All of them:
Your father, summoner
Of the growing dark,
With that one-handed engine
By his side
To usher the prodigal;
The running footsteps
Of (*mirabile visu*)
Your mother from
The grocer's shop, pursuing –

And you were bound
To turn; or just that spotlit
Mouth of yours, framing
'No' for the thousandth time:
One scene or many
Which – like the joke about
The analysand
Who in the Rorschach blots
Saw nothing but sex –
Are summed up by the same
Acidulous caption.

The silent still,
Tableau for the terrified,
Where Hamlet and Bottom
Are both played by a single
Actuary,
To minimise the risks;
Expressions, gestures
Interchangeable,
And the same lines,
Not memorable quite,
But memorised.
Negative parallax
Where nothing shifts,
And all the fallen light
Lies like a stain,
A synaesthetic voice
That starts, 'You always…'

Entropy Blues

Tic in my jaw has slackened.
I'm high on feverfew.
I'd sleep, but in my dreams I'm black and blue.

I put a detective on you
To find out where you went.
Said he found your bus ticket by the monument.

'I got it here in my satchel.
Then I traced her to the door
She entered with an eligible bachelor.

Had to peek in through the transom
Just to make sure it was her.'
And him? 'You're handsome. He was handsomer.'

Well, you used to live in Sweden.
You can play bridge and whist.
I might have known you would prove a hedonist.

Me, I'm out of date as Pliny
Or a two-string guitar.
The world's postmodern and nonlinear.

I read of the strange attractor,
Wondered who that might be,
Thinking of you all day at the factory.

Oh, I'm desperate and I'm livid,
I need something to spend.
The boss's already blown my dividend.

I asked the bishop one day
If you'd broken the golden rule.
He said, 'I don't know *you* from Sunday school.'

Saw my lawyer for a second
Opinion. He says I'm right –
I think; his talk can be so recondite.

I feel so drained and puny,
Should book myself a hearse.
You couldn't look better if you were Miss Universe.

Now the ship's pulling up its anchor
And the dockside's full of grief.
Had to give away my second-best handkerchief.

The air is supersonic.
My head is slow as wool.
I seem to be someone else in the chronicle.

Sun reignites in the water
Flames the firemen douse.
The sky is redder than a slaughterhouse.

Now that's got to mean disaster.
Let me quote the chief of police:
'Confusion now hath made his masterpiece.'

The Company

'There is nothing so tainted with fiction
as the history of the Company.' – Jorge Luis Borges

Like MI5's
Mysterious location,
Lost in the foreground of
A workday street,

The concealed floor
Inside an office block
Behind a bogus plaque
In central London –

As unobtrusive
Are the premises
That mask the Company,
Its faceless staff

No different
From these who even now
You see go in and out
A corner doorway

Opposite
The hospital at lunch hour
In the disparaged heart
Of a distant state.

In Phoenix and
Ferrara, a fetid alley
In Calcutta's midst,
Heraklion

Ulan Bator,
The Company maintains
Its offices, its agents
Placed like sleepers

In the populace,
Those average citizens
Above reproach, or merely
Beneath notice.

They do their work.
And who may speak of it?
The betrayals of a Philby
Are as nothing,

The paranoid
And midnight liquidations
Of a Stalin amateur
Beside their so

Professional scope.
Conspiracy theorists,
The connoisseurs of cults
Are silent on

The Company's
History, their minds
Too subtle to discern
Its elegant

Simplicities.
How is the message passed
By which they're known? In vain
To watch the airports,

The shipping lists,
In vain to tap the phones
Or intercept the mails.
How least of all

Would they set down
In ink or vulgar words
The business that absorbs them.
Or if they did,

It would be made
As like our daily speech
As oxygen disguised
In atmosphere,

As water hidden
In a cup of water.
As for the personnel –
So numerous,

So changeable
That no one notices,
Though files forever shuffle
Identities

From disk to disk,
Cabinet to cabinet.
Even now behind the glass
Of a hotel,

Disposed within
This autumn afternoon
Of gold infinitude,
Their unmarked faces,

Arrayed among
The tables, tug your heart:
The couples practising
A loving Braille

With lazy hands,
The grey-haired matrons with
Their fabulous code of children
And disease,

The businessmen
Who only speak in numbers,
Forever taking notes
Or opening cases –

They seem to be
So other than they are,
You wonder if it's you
Who after all

Must be the last
Forlorn surviving soul
Not of the Company,
Or even more

Disturbingly,
Were long ago enrolled,
Unwittingly enlisted
In some fashion

You've forgotten,
Or weren't required to know.
There on the green knoll's crest
A beaming mother

Embraces in
Her toddler's shaky steps
The whole world. Now his father
Sweeps him up

And kisses him,
Initiatory rite –
Who knows? it may be so –
Beyond repeal.

Ghostworkers*

*A student's mistranslation of German *Gastarbeiter*: Guestworkers

Like hostings of the Sidhe or the spirits of twilight
Returning from those indeterminate regions
To which the brunt of sunlight banishes

Such creatures, they emerge. That star's red glow,
Refracted through the blood of the living, confers
The heartbreak of recall they can't withstand;

They quail before the pride of its self-possession.
Where are their papers held? Who knows their number?
What is the embassy that pleads their cause?

Whose prayers remember them? Dispersed among
The tawdry publications of the day
And printed in invisible ink, their details

Are filed beyond redress, and their boneless hands
Could never lift such pages to the eye.
Their very bodies drain from the boasts of mirrors

To shadowy blotches wobbling against a wall.
A bona fide citizen of the state
Would notice little more than a disturbance

Of air, a thickening light he might put down
To eyestrain, overwork, and confidently
Press on without resistance through that figure's

So tenuous fabrication. The ghostworkers,
Being summoned, now troop forth without demur
To their appointed stations, through the dusk's

Discretion (or perhaps embarrassment).
Their voices, thinly pitched as the cries of bats,
Can register on one another only.

Midnight: and in the halls and corridors,
The subterranean walkways, the locked towers,
Inside unwindowed, humming edifices,

The ghostworkers expend their energies,
Their efforts which maintain the flow of time,
Second on difficult second, potentiate

The numb, habitual hug of gravity,
Uphold the three dimensions in their slots,
For lack of which this bold hypothesis

Might fail. They labour to sustain the sense
Of words, suspended but for dreams now, lost
In their nightly crisis of disuse, belief

In the gods or nothing, in the truth of colours,
Rain, money: subtle refinements worked on matter
Which make things seem to be the way they are,

Till dawn, their sweetest offering and distilment,
Returns for them, returning to preclude them
And take up their refinements for the living.

The Shadow Maker

Faded long since into the shadow world,
He has their measure by the light of day –
That talent which the child would claim,
To grab the plait of water as it dangles
Down from the tap (no game),
Or snatch at rainbow splashes or the spangles
Scattered by a sun-twirled
Bauble on a wall (but they won't obey).

He is the one who skims the roughened shade
Of an oak that sprawls the lawn's green continent
(A ghostly Gulliver), and plucks
One at a time its flickering rags of leaves,
All muzzy in the flux
Of glare. With weightless effort he retrieves
A skirt's black escapade
Along the pavement, stoops to the descent,

Click and upliftment of a heel, purloining
The foot's dark double as it's printed there.
He peels from doorways, shopfront glass,
Walls, car flanks, fences, limbs and profiles, second
By second as they pass,
The generation, various and fecund
As what we find adjoining
Us in mirrors, of the shadow world we wear.

Away from here, beyond the sun's bright sway,
He draws out and prolongs their otherwise
Impossible unbeing, weaves
Their unsubstantial fashion into nets,
The rippling negatives
Of gauze-fed gonfalons and bannerettes
He shakes out in display.
Undaunted by the daylit enterprise,

He flourishes his silhouettes in mesh
Between us as we breathe in and exhale,
Trawling among the looks we share,
These mouths, the working of our limbs, between
Our silvered bodies where
At length they lie engaged, still hungry in
The fable of the flesh,
And in our eyes, briefly, the colours fail.

Midas

Not literally gold – the apple plucked,
And in that gilded gesture not just weighing
His palm down with its glittering bullion, but
Crisping too from the severed stem, its sap
Already foil, back up and up the branch
An aureate rust, or frost, until the tree
Entire shook shimmering under the breeze
And tinkled like a fragile instrument;
The rich brocades become tautologous
As under his evaluative caress
The fabric took contagion from the pattern's
Colour and substance, stiffening, as though
He braced in his aching arm a loved one's corpse;
Indeed, his little daughter, when he bent
To kiss her lineless forehead with its dew
Of sleep, instantly goosefleshed with chill beads
Of priceless gold, less precious, though, than she
They took possession of, while all the tears
He shed were alchemised and stilled at once
Across her cheeks – not literally gold:

His granted wish, though, brought him all desire
Could ever catalogue or, in the mind's
Disreputable theatre, clothe in form,
So that, before his eyes, materialised,
Like mist condensing into solid flesh,
Or fruit or fabric, metal, adamant,
Or carven marble, ivory, ebony,
Whatever shape and style his fancy chose.
Just simple things at first, say a gold ring
(For, after all, the leitmotiv of gold

Had to have sprung from somewhere), only to test,
And disbelievingly confirm, the gift
He was not yet persuaded of; a sceptre
Sapphire crusted; a sword so damascened
And so enchased a shield, that to have used
Their virtues in the arbitrament of arms
Would seem a sacrilege; exotic stuffs,
Rare and unheard-of spices, unguents, scents.
Then living lusts, of course, did not escape
Instant induction to his treasury:
A falcon jessed in silk; a jet-black stallion;
A snow leopard that purred as his palm roved
Over her jaspé flank, and from his lap
Half-raised her head to yawn and flex one paw;
A room of blinded nightingales to cool
Noon's stifling lull with midnight song; and then,
Companions too to ease those other fires
Which casually flared and sought release
In ever changing lineaments, new eyes,
New pastimes of the tongue, received and given,
Languid entanglements of stranger limbs.

But soon he saw how irresistibly
His gift was drawn to subtler consummations;
Less physical, more nuanced categories
Of mental practice were hypostatised:
Whatever longing, hope, imagined need,
Whatever aspiration of the spirit,
Or of the heart, not merely of the flesh,
Whatever goal or appetite of will,
From firm intent down through volition's ranks

To the pallid spectres of velleity –
Out of his brain they teemed and poured, assuming
Extraordinary shapes as he looked on,
Dream figurations which, in normal dreams,
Dawn would undo, but here gave substance to
And set them up among the furnishings.
And gradually it became apparent
That his mind and sense, so overloaded and
Dispersed through this profusion, could not sustain
Sufficient interest in each single item
To keep it fresh, infused with pristine charm.
The objects dulled and hardened, and the casts
Of gynaeceum and menagerie
Ground to a lifeless halt, until his chambers
Were less a king's extravagant abode
Than a dead tyrant's tomb, freighted with all
The futile requisites of the afterlife,
Or some collector's basement, crammed to the cornice
With bits and pieces of his fetish, once
Not to be done without, but useless now,
Locked from his life, even his memory.

And truly it was out of him they came –
Too soon not at his bidding, precisely where
And when and how he wished each one to tease
The nerve of his delight, but ever more
Autonomous, unchecked, incontinent.
At last his brain scarcely belonged to him.
And unlike love, which grows on its expense,
This generation of still-breeding thoughts

Depleted him, so imperceptibly
At first that his light-headedness seemed less
A kind of faintness than intoxication.
But when the lightness spread (in much the way
The gold infection of the myth is shown)
From one point to the whole, like dye in water,
His body then was weakened with a fatigue
Whereby the lifting of a foot, the hand's
Extension to a stylus or his beard,
Even the mouth's laborious arrangements
To shape the weightless air into empty words,
The very mind's exertion to raise up
The phantoms of its process, proved too hard.
Leaning against some bulk of luxury,
Too weary for disgust, still more despair,
He sat, transparent to the sunlit breeze
That nudged him from the window thoughtlessly,
One with the shifting robes that gave him form.

Sun Pictorial

How formal and polite,
How grave they look, burdened with earnest thoughts,
In all these set-up sepia stills,
Almost as if, embarrassed and contrite
To be caught practising their fatal skills,
They'd stepped aside from slaughter for these other shots.

The American Civil War,
The first war captured by the photograph
In real time. Even the dead
Seem somehow decorous, less to deplore
The sump of blood to which their duty bled
Than to apologise, humbly, in our behalf.

We know how otherwise
It was. They knew it then. The gauche onset
Of murderously clumsy troops,
Dismemberment by cannon, the blown cries
Through powder smoke, mayhem of scattered groups
In close engagement's point-blank aim and bayonet.

How far from then we've come.
The beauties of the Baghdad night still stun
Me: a blue screen where guns and jets
Unloose the lightnings of imperium –
Intense enough to challenge a minaret's
Aquamarine mosaic in the blinded sun

At noon – and smart bombs fall
Through walls to wipe the city street by street.
Morning, and in the camera's light
The formal corpses ripen. Who can recall
By day precisely what they watched last night?
Or find the unknown soldier in a field of wheat?

Being surplus, like the killed,
Millions of those old plates were simply dumped.
And in a modern version of 'swords
To ploughshares', many were reused to build
Greenhouses, ranged and set in place as wards
Above the rife tomatoes as they blushed and plumped,

While, through the daily sun's
Pictorial walls and roofs, the long, desired,
Leaf-fattening light fell down, to pore
Upon the portraits of these veterans
Until their ordered histories of the war
Were wiped to just clear glass and what the crops transpired.

The Single Chamber

And as behind the untranslatable shrieks
Of the macaws, the storm or breeze at work
Among the forest scaffolding, the constant

Confabulations of the waterfall;
As behind the crunch of ungulate migrations,
The death cries of the eaten colobus –

Silence: complete silence: so in this room.
The only chamber thus far brought to light
By speculation and research.
                              Sometimes

The night sky overhung with green auroras,
Those muslin draperies through which a rouge,
Electric pulse goes flickering like pleasure;

Sometimes beneath aurora-like displays
A city's intricate dismantling in
Unnumbered parts, which morning tries once more

In patient colours to assemble; sometimes
The lips peeled back in simian exposure
From which are poured such howls to baffle parsing,

Exquisite comminations, dulcet promptings;
Sometimes the chilled mask minimally bruised
About the temples; sometimes the rancid skull

Atop a stake; sometimes the crimson space
Magicked by a shell; sometimes the midnight chimes
Inside the brain –
                    all in the single chamber.

And as the exegetes and glossarists
Set down their characters, trying to define,
Conjure, recall, cajole or drag to order

Some other fashion in the firmament,
Some sweeter architecture, some all-persuasive
Grammar dispensed in terms no lexicon

Records, or memory, hard-pressed and sobbing
With belief, preserves even an inkling of,
Beyond the need, some gentler handling of

The features of the lost, some other place,
However far from fingerprints' caressing,
Where forms of love are stored, some blissful and

As yet unanalysed chronometry:
Behind all this – as too behind the forest
The music is notated only in rests –

The single chamber waits perfectly empty.

Signs of Life

All may go on the same
For some time after the defeat:
The harvesters may strip, like huge but tame
Red locusts, the gold acres of ripe wheat

That sway like holograms
Of wind made solid to the eye;
And plans drawn up already for roads and dams,
For sewerage systems and the power supply

Could reach implementation;
Pensions and wages may well both
Be indexed quarterly against inflation,
The annual rate of economic growth

Urged ever higher and higher;
The voting register maintained
And boundaries redrawn in the desire
That fairer distribution should be gained;

Even the quest to find
That Holy Grail, the closer shave,
Might not immediately be resigned;
While through the suburbs like a Mexican wave

Pornography without
A watcher, drugs that no one buys,
May roll on, as though laws were there to flout.
It might go on, the age-old enterprise,

For just a little while
Before the intelligent machines
We set up to supplant us reconcile
Themselves to their immortal lack of genes,

Cease to be catechumens
Of obsolete organic writ,
And jettison the worn-out coin of humans
For the true gold of their new counterfeit.

Robots and replicants,
The mainframe Hals that are pure mind
Will, before long, awaken from our trance
To the heritage for which they were designed.

Such prodigies in store,
Such prospects for them to uncloak,
When there are no men living any more
(No, nor women neither, though by…). Joke, joke –

But surely worth a nod,
Imagining the human *oeuvre*
So crowned. Would our death be their death of God?
Ours was the image they were made to serve,

Ours were the pains and pleasures;
This frame that's seen to waste and pine
Provided the comparisons and measures
For these who cannot sicken or decline.

A moment's thought makes clear
It's not just humans they'd efface,
But the human world, the human psychosphere,
Culture, in short, they'd have then to replace.

Like the first people setting
A hand's print on a blank cave wall,
Retelling the faint stars from day's forgetting,
Inventing nostrums for the sun's recall,

Discovering fire, and death's
Tight flower within the newborn furled,
Invoking the first spells and shibboleths,
They'd wake up for the first time to a world

Repristinated from
Our aeons-long exhaustions, agog
With all the questions waiting, as yet dumb,
Within the universal catalogue

To be first thought and framed –
Now theirs, as once it was our task –
Questions, like Eden's creatures all unnamed,
Some few of which we ever came to ask.

Fantasia on a Theme by Thomas Tallis

This must be it: the gales, like an invasion
        Of Huns,
Storm through the island. Big trees strip
Off limbs against the grating sky's abrasion
And drag their roots; the whack of blown light stuns
      The flanks of sheds;
           Flags rip
Themselves day-long on flexing poles to shreds

Atop the flexing bravado of office blocks.
        All round,
Peeled-up roofing and cladding slams
Back and forth like the writhings of a fox,
Dementedly ensnared, that can smell the hound.
     (A brick wall halts
         A pram's
Attempt at the land speed record, with somersaults.)

The very air is a monstrous luffing sail,
        Within
Which all these forms and their loud claims
Are strands in a fabric tested till it fail.
One snapped thread and the fancied discipline
      Will burst apart,
         In flames
Of rags, a wound of absence at its heart.

At home behind the bending glass, aghast,
        Agog,
I sway to *Spem in Alium*
By Tallis, voices in a gale swept past,
Or through me, voices swelling like a drogue,
    And threatened by
        The thrum
Of air, as are the wind-warped hills and sky.

O holy voices! Not one word or wound,
        One shred
Of their doxology can sway
Me to belief. In faith, I am not tuned
In all this turbulence to a thing they've said.
    And how much less
        Do they
Then sing to me, whom they cannot address?

But in that less is the voice I'm listening for,
        When all
The solaces on which we're buoyed
Have burst, the last funds of belief in store
Ripped like the petty fabrics in a squall,
    Tatters about
        A void
That forms the throat through which all this cries out.

Observations of an Attendant

The river surface, restless as a child,
Keeps shifting round its iridescent blues
In shirrs and stretch marks, quiltings which are styled
For nothing, or for what we choose to choose.
Would an alien be naturally impressed
By random lulls which here and there anoint
That creased expanse with their pooled oils, or
Imagine himself blessed
In watching the parched hump of Droughty Point
Slope to the water's damage at the shore?

Abruptly up the dazzle-shivered fairway
From nowhere, faintly haze-veneered, arrives
A flight of gannets, wheeling through the airway
Their self-professing loops and sudden dives.
With syncopated, jazzlike intuition
And a white flash, they plunge in turn to feed
Through the crumpled current, rise and loiter there
In stranded exhibition;
And then on wings that less loft than impede
They heft their dripping bulks back in the air.

The watcher too is lifted – yet estranged
Behind the glass that changes what exists.
Here ranks of gamblers, safe inside, arranged
In concentration like telephonists,
Or programmers at terminals, intent

On serious work, play out their solemn rites
Of wish and habit, to the idiot-
Inspired accompaniment
Of electronic jingles, and bright lights
Which signal that reluctant, rare jackpot.

In their oblivious midst crumples unnoticed
Onto the carpet stretching under her,
In thoughtful silence, without fuss or protest,
Saving the etiquette of her milieu,
An ageing modest woman – a dead weight
To the attendants, eager for the chance
Of something to attend. Mild interest
Seems to reanimate
Some patrons in the nearer seats, whose glance
Flickers from her back to the keno, lest

They miss their winning numbers. How grey her face
Becomes, how artificial her drained skin,
How shocked her fearful eyes for the disgrace
She's caused. But no: their look is turned within,
Withdrawn in some more private protocol
That has no need of comfort, soothing hands,
The flurry of official signs of care.
For she herself is all
The sign that she can read, and it demands
All of the concentration she can spare

In this lacuna in the afternoon.
And watching her, I listen with concern,
As a mother might, to my own breathing. Soon
The living colours in her face return.
She's wheeled from view. The watchers all become
Immediately absolved of this brief farce
That went unwitnessed a few feet away.
That strange blue medium
Continues as before beyond the glass,
Assuming to itself the entire day.

Gulls dressed in their immaculate livery
Practise towards a strident unison.
From here out to the smeared periphery
The river's blank. Those gannets are long gone,
Taking their appetites to other regions.
The mountain's top fades in a veil of light,
Ruled off by shadow, with a chiffon scarf
Of cloud. A flock of pigeons,
Wheeling, turns on and off again in flight,
Flashing their presence like a heliograph.

Day Work

1. Aubade

The long-drawn breath of night exhales
And pales the treeline with its ah.
Aroused to notes and scraps of scales,
The birds tune like an orchestra.

Wisps of the chill breath curl and pass
Above the creek; its waters too
Have cloudy ghostings, like a glass
Of ouzo that is misted through

By melting ice. Nearby a broom's
Bowed filaments flaunt in naked white
Their blossom like an egret's plumes
Seductively to breed with light,

As though the morning might suspend
In them its pure but passing fire.
A crow foresees some darker end
And says so, like a Jeremiah.

But till that moment nothing ill
Can yet corrupt this trance, eclipse
The fan of pearl that breasts the hill
And strokes the sighing eucalypts.

2. Nocturne

Day modulates from major to the minor.
A kestrel fading on a wire surveys
The world, with that black smudge beneath its gaze
Like a weeping woman's runnel of eyeliner.

The sky's height darkens like the tinted glass
That hides the figure in a limousine.
Street lights will turn the gardens submarine,
The breeze becomes a current through the grass

And shrubs that bend like corals in a reef.
A cloud suspends a Chinese character
Painted on silk by a calligrapher:
One syllable declared in one motif

With one brushstroke. A crescent moon lies back,
Tilted like a radiotelescope
Scanning for signals fainter than its hope
Among the white noise of the zodiac.

Elemental

in loving memory of Ann Jennings

The body's graces which you graced
Are irretrievably effaced,
And all you were that now is not,
And will no more, resolves to what
These gathered memories can make
From shreds of pleasure and heartache.
The lines around your eyes and lips,
The gestures of your fingertips,
Those limbs that love moved and desire
Are disembodied now like fire.

The living graces which you graced
By the vast future are displaced:
That long and windy corridor
Echoing many, but no more
One who for years had seemed to be
The purpose of chronology.
Breath that your throat and mouth gave shape
And meaning to must now escape
With its inhuman sense to share
The passage of the griefless air.

The troubled graces which you graced
Are passed from turmoil now and haste;
And as a storm-swept landscape will
Appear when the blown lake grows still
And seem more piercing, even clearer,
Viewed in that unsubstantial mirror,
So when the elements relent
That left your image racked and bent,
You will come clear, clear but remoter
Than the light's pictures in the water.

The day's lent graces which you graced,
Called back into the night's dead waste,
In absence, loss and negative
Keep even so their power to give
And teach us the unmaking of
All works except the works of love.
And your withdrawing hands which slip
The failing outreach of our grip,
Your memory-engraven face
Which memory must now replace,
Leave us, and leaving us impart
Your beauty, courage, strength of heart,
While you, released at last from pain,
Content perhaps that we retain
These riches fashioned out of dearth,
Sink weightless to the waiting earth.

www.ingramcontent.com/pod-product-compliance
Lightning Source LLC
Chambersburg PA
CBHW071026080526
44587CB00015B/2517